Bukowski Charm

Trash Fire Poetry to Warm the Soul

Ty Gardner

Copyright © 2020 by Ty Gardner

Cover art copyright © 2020 by Shelly Gardner

All rights reserved. No part of this publication may be reproduced, stored in a retrieval system, or transmitted in any form or by any means, electronic, mechanical, photocopying, recording, or otherwise without written permission of the copyright owner except for the use of quotations in a book review.

For more information, address: gardnty@gmail.com

ISBN: 9798673097144

Write a thing. An anything. An Everything. Sinew your vows to humanity by way of words and serve your brothers and sisters. Know your hands to the walls of the castle of this kingdom on earth and write a thing. An anything. An everything.

Table of Contents

Dreamscape Love Affair	11
Blizzards 'n Hell Hound Howls	12
Depot Musings	13
Poesy Prosy	14
Who Am I to Speak of Dreams?	15
As If	16
Bukowski Charm	17
Of Babbling Brooks and Veiled Canopies	18
I Thought, I Thought, I Knew	19
Judas, We Hardly Knew Thee	20
Keepers' of the Light	21
The Fever State	22
Exit Stage Left	23
Rearview Mirror Eyes	24
A Place of Dust and Campfire Smoke	25
Songs of Discarded Furniture	26
An Ode to Youth and Creeks	27
Exercises in Existentialism	28
A Funny Story About a Broken Nose	29
The Secret Dreams of Shadows	30
Funny, Ain't It? Ain't It?	31
Apple Pie Americana	32
Say, "Cheese"	33

On the Precipice of the Golden Hour	34
Some Kind of Cool	35
Thinking About Thinking	36
The Day I Turned My Back on God	37
Tales of an Idaho Youth	38
Shallow Graves of Poe-prosed Lore	40
Cloud Migration Taught Me About Death	41
Two-Tones and Working Drones	42
A Paradox of Potential and Possibilities	43
The Silence in Lands of Waste and Sage	44
Weeping Heart Love Story	45
A Saga of Sand and Exile	46
Faces of Wonderland Avenue	47
Back, Before	48
Roundabout Lovers	49
Desert Highway Deliberations	50
Morning Dawn O'er Walden Pond	51
In Meadows Gold	52
Ig•ner•uh ns is Ignorance	53
Tumult-love Tornado	54
Things I Don't Laugh About	57
An Homage to Forgotten Particles of Driftwood	58
We're Sitters, We	60

The Way I Know My, Love	61
Balloon Sky	62
Mood Swings of City Streets	63
Cyclical Salvation	64
The Last Drop of Cherry Blooms	65
Corporate the Giant	66
I Don't Know This Skin and Bones	67
The Age of Panacea	68
Seasons of Neon Nightmare	69
An Open Letter to Simpler Things	70
Communication Stock Exchange	71
Alight the Silken Blades of Rye	72
Leona's Story	74
The Rainey Street Wrangler	75
The Sounds of Settled Dust	76
Siren Songs of Rambling Roads	77
Barking Songs of Sea Lions	78
That Night We Danced	79
The Nihilists'	80
Poetry in Pinecone Dust	81
In Monochrome Dreams	82
Steel Track Tramps	83
Same As It Ever Was	84

When I Think on Donna	85
September's Parting	86
Mrs. Van Winkle	87
Freight Train Trespasses	88
The Silences Between	89
A Courtship of Drifters	90
A Penny for Your Sense	92
Concentric Love	93
The Scriptures of Wise Waters	94
Life Between	96
Kindness in the Soft Lines	97
Kill Hole Conundrum	98
Cigarettes in the Shadows	99
Of the Things I'll Miss Most	100
Square Sides of 'Round Love	102
Alieni Generis	103
I Couldn't Save My Sons, Myself	104
In the Firm Grip of Fir Trees	105
On the Last Day	106
Acknowledgments	109
About the Author	111

Dreamscape Love Affair

Although I never truly knew her, I loved her in words.
Hid traces of her in plain view and spattered her like
stars across the night sky in the aesthetic of my work.
Let her wear me as layers of cheap abuse
and sailed oceans wide in cotton candy ships to please.
I brooded, as they boiled and brimmed,
emotions that run hot and flow over.

Itching.
Scratching.
Clawing.

Fingering at the festering space of deprival.
Such deprival.
I'd never felt so deprived.
But there's no finer dining than the female form.
Their bends and curves are a bible verse, and I longed redeeming.

Hoping.
Praying.

Wishing to keep her in words and not the nightmare in notes
I'd come to dream about: the whistling tune of Twisted Nerves that floated
dreamily beneath the chorus of
heel-clack echoes—sounds of impending doom.
To keep her, white-picket-fences-and-manicured-lawns-happy,

I loved her in words.

Blizzards 'n Hell Hound Howls

'S blinding blizzards what brought 'em in;
cold as polar bear paws 'n twice as sharp.
Smarted cheeks 'n rubbed raw the lid skin of thare eyes it did.
Let in a turrible draft when they broke through the bolted and boarded
barn style door—winds wilder 'n hell hound howls.

Depot Musings

Rapt of a woe-taled mourning sun melancholy,
I'd mused at the marvel of life beyond the malevolence
of a terra-thick murk.
Weighted as the burden of loss, thick like a heart
overcome with grief, I'd mused.
Mused at the wonder of something that could amaze me,
the way stars hang low o'er paradise lost,
something akin a fallen Angel's foreshadowing
of reigning Hell riches surmounting salvation through servitude.
Something... ritual, maybe, in the erring of old Adam,
weep-eyed and weary of boot-sly serpents the way they dangled,
bandit-handed burglars and bad guys, perhaps,
profligates to the powers that be, but treated as royals
by the penny-pinched and impoverished.
Doffed-cap scalps and curtsy'd-skirts hung low when
crossing paths with those thug-crowned kings, I'd mused.

Poesy Prosy

With wind-whipped cheeks, atop the high peaks,
the sunrise I've met with a smile.

Though the scale to that crest demanded my best,
I'd have not traded feet for the mile.

And thus this is true, in all that we do,
our plight to exceed all our flaws.

Stay strong, carry on, till your time here is gone;
may betterment be your life cause.

Who Am I to Speak of Dreams?

Stack them in corners, the awful things I've said.
Pressed pages worn and waterlogged,
a towering tribute to tears and torment.
Let winds of baying sorrow-storms blow them asunder.
Me, in the marrow of it, whimpering inaudibly into the deafening fury.
For who am I to speak of dreams?
To plead spiritedly the plight of lassoed-moons and sons a-flight to suns.
Who am I to marvel reveries of a world
transcended by the power of my thoughts?
As if I, of modest means and plain dress,
receding in tussock-grays, could perform such a trick.
The mountains of the world never fussed much when asked to move,
but should I have demanded as much of my own sons?
A father knows better but forgets himself.
It's just simpler than admitting that we're spiders,
tall as skyscrapers cowering in a corner,
keeping quiet about our complex conversations
with Madness and the rainbow history of the cosmos laid before us.
Cowering and reflecting the vibrancy of its tones, knowing that, within
the depths of insanity lie the brushstroke of clarity.
So stack them in corners, the awful things I've said.
Who am I to speak of dreams?

As If

I was asked once, of the Plaths' and Dylans' of the world.
Of their intimate understanding of the soul
and how they knew which words would carry the most weight.

Asked, as if sermons of changing times in dustbowl desert towns
and elders who preached on deaf ears of a dying sun were nothing
more than the nonsensical squabbling of salon patrons between gossip
magazine gawking.

Asked, as if the notion of bristled-lip sunscreen barons and the creditors of
dreams on layaway, were as sensible to the layman as torrent-skies bound
for Kansas.

Asked, as if the taste of fire were a topic of regular conversation
between mothers of plastic smiles, and her dinner table dismissives with
their eyes glued to squawk-boxes and 'smart' devices.

Asked, as if such things could be so easily explained, as if there were no
questions left unanswered.

Bukowski Charm

Where thunder meets the lightning rain,
a place of little pauses, like the calming of commas,
keeping run-ons from running off through the wildlands
of lost thoughts, come to me.

Where aged oaks splinter and split, give way to gravity and gift themselves
back to the ground, find me.

In shallow graves of repurposed words,
little catacombs of calumny where weeds and fescue
can take root and run wild (something of a hollow, wide as an open range
so that all the senseless sentences can be pipered into catatonia), muse me.

Come, find and muse me thoughts of marooning ourselves in the soft
spaces between waves of Neruda's words,
of casting our lines into oceans of Bukowski charm to see what comes up.

Muse me small sighs of packing our bags,
putting out our thumbs and placing it all on the line,
skint as the skin of our teeth—Kerouac style.

Find me there and mouth the words, "what if?"

Of Babbling Brooks and Veiled Canopies

Veiled of crowned canopies, bespeckled by
d
r
o
p
s
of luminosity playfully peeking through the slightest apertures,
I respite contentedly of all worldly strife.
There is a tranquility here, in the sprawling greenery
of this recreational world, and the tumultuous buzz of the aggregation just
beyond these hallowed grounds becomes nothing more than a dull hum;
the murmur of a babbling brook.
A slight breeze rises up to greet me with a rapturous embrace as I close
my eyes to reflect the halcyon of my youth.
The sighs of the swaying branches overhead expound on the
greater mysteries of life, and I am apprised anew
of the magnificence of this world.
No simpler pleasures have my heart and mind found solace than this.

I Thought, I Thought, I Knew

I thought, I thought, I knew pain.
How it weighs objectively.
Coils a heart concretely and pulls...

elsewhere.

Somewhere.

Anywhere.

Thought maybe living meant outlasting it.
But that just meant outliving love;
knowing new pain, old pain anew.

I thought, I thought, I knew.

Judas, We Hardly Knew Thee

On broken backs and crook-kinked necks they danced confetti dust.
The pitter-pattering of their raindrop heartbeats echoed a melancholy
madness adrift to the stars, and those who could not join were woeful.
The petrichor of their fallen tears was intoxicating.
It was the summer of the great discontent,
and all the trees were blossoming snow flakes.

From sandcastle windows we waved our goodbyes to those who danced,
ocean waves nipping our feet in the ticka-tocka rhythm
of silt washing away to sediment-fate.
We'd betrayed the light of revelation, lived a lifetime in eye-blink glances
before the fall, and the hunting season would soon be upon us.

(Run, rabbit, run. We simply can't wear dirty boots to bed.)

It was the summer of the great discontent,
and all the trees were blossoming snow flakes.

Keepers' of the Light

True what they say, there's an enchantment in the light.

Keeps 'em's keepers' wide-eyed and terrified to look away.

Keeps the slosh and waves of the sea in a northernly wind it does.

Traps 'em's keepers' souls bound to the body of gulls, squawk-beaked and blister-eyed, the light.

The Fever State

In a fevered state, I found myself stolen far above the splendor
of a palatial mountain valley.
The rolling foliage unraveling below me was lush and vast,
and I found the whole of it to be completely untouched
by the influence of men.
Of a dark brown plumage, I did soar upon thermal currents,
spying all manner of creatures from inconceivable distances.
But of these things I paid no mind.
My time here would soon come to a close,
and I resolved to regard the majesty of this place in its entirety.
Whence I would come again, I could not say.
And by the glow of the setting sun, I carried on.

Exit Stage Left

It's au revoir and curtains, love;
a stage left swan song and sorrow-eyed 'so long' I fear.
A break-a-leg-goodbye and
two-left-feet-toodle-oo it seems, love—Godspeed-and-goodnight-curtseys
to audiences adrift in adoration.
No lines left now, love, to improvise or learn.
No fealty, to amber-waxed and dusted love story letters
of first spark fireworks and suitcase stashed stock
card tales of big band ballroom hoopla,
highway diner anecdotes and road trip quips
down Route 66—attic refuse of an Americana
we fought to protect, no fealty.
Aye, no grandeur left to behold, love,
of a dew-seeped mountain floor morn;
how it breathes kaleidoscope waves of scents and
sounds in the still of steady silence.
To have stood in the dust of the history of the earth's flavors,
letting them carry you aloft to the heavens, no grandeur.

Rearview Mirror Eyes

I caught a glimpse of it once, the love he felt for me,
in the weighted glance of his rearview mirror eyes.

I was but a boy then but I think on it often;
the kindness reflecting back at me like floating
lanterns against the night sky.

A Place of Dust and Campfire Smoke

Come hell or high water come and gone,
came and went, went and left 'em high and dry—without a paddle
and no place to hang their hats.
Replaced by reeds and rushes now,
the rushing of rain water sent 'em runnin',
sent 'em seeking a source of new shelter someplace else.
A sweet spot, between cotton tuft and tree petal budding,
somewhere on the backside of time where snow and
pine and peace and quiet are a picture of perfection.
Where all the pretty horses roam, that's where they longed to be.
Where painted palominos pounded the open
plains and the muscled thighs of mustangs gleamed
sweat in the midnight moons of desert heat.
To breathe dust and campfire smoke,
to drink and weave themselves in poetry
before being too old to know better,
and telling themselves they won't become like those before them,
they longed to be.

Songs of Discarded Furniture

I remember it being this way, the pageantry of it.
Long before we were married to songs of discarded
furniture under freeway overpasses and the silt settled in my bones.
When late night talks of life and loving at the furthest edges
of the earth made their way into the small hours.

How we talked then.
Smiled at the thought of falling away into the universe, gliding idly
through star currents and making our home in the soft tones
of the moon's smile.

How we pulled at each other's wildest inhibitions then.
Slapped and screamed and smashed our bones together just
to see what chemistry we'd make; danced an incantation under
w v s
  a e
of silken sheet, listening through bated breath
to the history of all things in the epos of the sun.

How we did it all then...

But somewhere along the line we got [wrapped] up in the blanket of life.
It's any night of the week and I should be somewhere else.
The kids' are all dancing to songs I listened to at their age.

An Ode to Youth and Creeks

An ode,
to splashed-creek river bottoms—rock bed ballads of composed corrosion.
To compositions of stone, smoothed by the stratagems of time and tide,
bleach-brindled by the span of a sun's cycle;

cyclical, consistent, steady as calendars.

An ode,
to youth and creeks.
To slow drive sliding into b-side stories of being eighteen again.
Back when, before back when was even a passing thought.
Long before long agos' and being lost in reflection,
when we pushed the boundaries of originality.
Before the reserved silence, trodding in tumbled-twos
'long the tracks the long way 'round.
Before time was ticking away, tocking us into things
in a roundabout direction, directing us back, full circle.
Knowing the game, winning, wasting our time, ticking and grinning.

Exercises in Existentialism

I once believed that I knew, that I didn't even know,
that I didn't know that I didn't know.
But what do I know?
I am but a particle in the great subterfuge.
A constituent of the objective realities of my plane of existence.
But just how confident am I of the authenticity of these collectives?
And by what mechanisms does one even use to form these authentications?
Could I demonstrate those truths unequivocally if I were somehow
enlightened to the mechanics of those methods?
To what ends would such awareness
be useful in the landscape of cognitive dynamics?
A burgeoning state of madness blankets the mind at the very thought of it.
That I may never fully understand how subjective the subjects that
constitute my subjectivity are, perpetuates a state of restiveness that cannot
be suppressed save for one thing:
a complete and total catharsis of the existential mentality.
I must resolve to find satisfaction in the unknown
that I might eschew myself as the orchestrator of my own demise.

A Funny Story About a Broken Nose

Funny, 'bout a broken nose,
the crook of it once you've cocked off one too many times.
Funny, how damage done can deviate the septum,
part the passages and put a pause on breathing.
Funny, that we're physical that way, fisticuff pompous
when we're pushed past our point, that pinprick pinch that pulls you in,
wool-eyed and dog-whistle-deaf with delusion—madness in inked-green
gluttony and Godless greed like pressed-suit pretension to grease the heels
that slip slowly into a facsimile flavored you.
And there's no way forward going back once it's broken;
no fossiled-footstep paths to circle round
and mend the fractured fences of your thunder-hooved youth.
Best to let 'em lie, the sleeping-dogged
steel-cold codswallop cruelty of your lesser self.
Best to soldier onward, ever onward.

The Secret Dreams of Shadows

Andromeda bound by way of clustered cosmos,
we reel in motion—perpetual hurtling through
stages of change, cycles and phases.
Of Elysian fields we dare to dream.
Dare to hope of daring to dream.
But it is within the daring to hope that we navigate away from our dreams.
We find ourselves instead, deep in the vast wastelands of a desert we can't
quite recall the name of.
Find ourselves at what appears to be a sort of amalgamation of worlds;
a seam conjoining the very fabric of our earthly home,
and a parallel universe comes to mind.
A place we can only describe as something akin to a sensation, or feeling.
We hear ourselves thinking aloud,
what can be said, when asked of one's shadow?
Of formalities between us, friend or foe.
Do they speak of secrets, quietly, with other shadows?
Can it be said they stay with us in the shade, strumming silently,
air guitar euphonies as we weigh the heft of our decisions?
Do they, too, dare to hope of daring to dream?

Funny, Ain't It? Ain't It?

Life is funny, man.
Fickle, festering, foliage—overgrowth of you were,
you are, and you will be.

But how do we presume to know the first thing
about the first thing of things?
Of being human and fostering humanity towards our fellow who-mans?

Life is funny...

Apple Pie Americana

Keep a weather eye for the ruby butterfly
a-perch the plum blossom pinks of his Orient haven.
Where sweetgrass fields a-bud 'longside glacial spring runoff
and mountain folk are the knob-topped and cloven-hooved tenants
of the ceiling of the world.

Parables of poets who've pondered the cosmos, puzzled the meaning
of life and our purpose, are scribed in the inked-edges of his wings.
Ciphers and symbols of the great secrets, tales of the orchard days of our
mother's mothers'—the halcyon days of window-silled scents in apple pie
Americana and bluegrass banjo bouquets, bait and tackle blue-water bayou
boat rides and campfire cookout kumbayas, in the inked-edges.

Say, "Cheese"

The clocks are moving faster now, I thought I had more time.
Thought forever lived in Polaroid printouts and
merry-go-round merriment—banalities of playground pleasantries.

Never knowing I'd know the flavor of hair dye,
I thought I had more time.

On the Precipice of the Golden Hour

Amidst the flaxen glow of mountain fields,
my hands alight the feathered antithesis, I glide contentedly.
It is here, on the precipice of the golden hour,
the playful touch of the west wind lightly splaying the acquiescence
of my surroundings to and fro, that I regard the resplendence
of the twilight before me bringing to a close,
another in a long succession of rhythms in my hallowed earthly existence.

I have lived a hundred lifetimes in that space,
my visage aglow those radiant evening beams.
Oh that I might know a thousand more before the
horizon irrevocably parts me of that resplendence
and I am veiled eternally of the great dark.

Some Kind of Cool

    James Dean rebel,
she wore that crooked smile like a black leather jacket.

Baby,

    you were some kinda cool,

and I blew it.

Thinking About Thinking

Might've been the way she laced her shoes;
the wide berth swoop and loop of her shoelace
that was sure to make me snicker each time.
The way her converse high tops could be a
conversation always got me thinking.
Thinking about faith in rainwater, a cleansing thing.
The way it sings sermon songs to the soul.
Thinking about the way I'm content with
sun-peeked clouds—winked-hellos from the softer side of storms.
Thinking how we held our babes with cupped-heart hands.
Carried them, sheet-swathed and swaddled, quieting our tears,
blinking them back with cheek-close confidence and cradling them.
Thinking of conversations of love and why we yearn
for ocean-starred skies at night.
The little things, in the way she laced her shoes,
that always got me thinking.

The Day I Turned My Back on God

Denied it in the Shanghai streets,
the hand of God to pull me up and out of dirt-tide times.
Thought myself too suave for the healing balm of the
savior and cast my blind eyes to the sun.
Prayed instead to see the light in the snapshot-photoed past I'd left behind.

Tales of an Idaho Youth

I.

High in the jutting mountain ranges of southeastern Idaho,
a touch shy of the Great Divide along the Montana state line,
lie the wonderment of Henry's Lake;
a shallow blanket of sparkling blue water encircled cozily of
the dazzling Lionhead mountains to the east.

It was here, in the heartlands of our ancestors that my relatives
and I spent a great and many summer afternoons
aboard my grandfather's boat angling resolutely,
our hearts abounding with hopes of netting the ideal catch.

II.

Fondly I recall those summer vacations to my grandfather's Teton home,
voyaging endlessly along the woodland roads of Island Park as we made
our way to that enchanted reservoir.

Higher and higher we climbed, eventually breaking free
of the surrounding density, crossing the threshold
of a resplendent prairie-world enchanted of sprawling meadows,
lush vegetation, and meandering streams
giving way lazily to slumbering pools.

Even now, despite the steady passing of time,
I behold the arresting beauty of those lands
as vividly and serenely in my memories,
as I did at the height of those carefree childhood ventures.

III.

And how I do miss those ventures into the rolling hills
of the Caribou-Targhee forests, the cooling mist
of the lake water as it pushed up and past the bow of our boat to greet us,
and the hearty chuckle of my grandfather as he scooped up our
glimmering golden trophies from their aquatic environs.

Oh that I could once again be overcome with the exhilaration that comes
from the explosive pull of a mighty cutthroat,
dashing wildly to and fro in frenzied desperation to break free the rod.

My heart pines to relive those sacred moments,
but alas, the time of my father's father has passed,
and those bygone moments are nothing more than spirits of another life.

Shallow Graves of Poe-prosed Lore

I'd heard their calls from down below;
from shallow graves in Poe-prosed lore.
From pine box palls I heard their pleas,
the blood curdling blaring of banshees bawling down below.

With trowel-hands I burrowed,
bent on saving them from bridging worlds.
From bones and dust.
From words draped in fettered garb,
candy-coated and sweet to glorify the favored flavor for sip-slurp
swallowing an empire wrought with bone-gum rot.

Burrowed, to free them from smiles of wolves with tallow chins,
shifty eyes and crooking grins—grifter-cheeked scalawags.

Burrowed, to lay them bare, shadowed-qualms of sheeted-ghosts
and fog-washed highways;
helium-hand-hallucinations of feeble-framed constitution, I burrowed.

Cloud Migration Taught Me About Death

How childish and lonely to realize the migration
of clouds—a haunting epoch of self-awareness and clarity.

I think I knew it then; the truth of my mortality.

Forming from nothing, sunshine and peace.

Building then billowing, rage and rain.

Dissipating, faded and final.

Two-Tones and Working Drones

Finger-gun poppin' pistoleros, we were lithe;
rip-roaring and ready to rock 'em and sock 'em.
We've gone the way of two-tones and working
drones since then, but man we had it.
Modern music isn't the same without power chords,
and these kids don't want their MTV.

A Paradox of Potential and Possibilities

I've a mind attune the insipid drear of a winter lull today.
A low fog masks the high peaks,
lightly seasoning their rigid tops with a dash of white.

And so it is within, slate-gray skies have stolen over me,
and brought with them an indomitable chill.
I am suffused of a hard and bitter frost,
and find my inclinations apathetic in nature.
Oh that the sun could penetrate this rolling gloom
and soften me of this hostile incursion.
For I am not now who I once was, nor am I who I will be.
I am a duality of both wasted potential, and infinite possibilities.
I am the paradox of an old ship having all of its parts and pieces
completely replaced while staying the same
and becoming something else entirely.
I am alive without having previously existed in my life,
and I have also yet to live, and the parallel
between, 'who I am,' and 'who am I?'
cannot one without the other run its course.

Because despite our best laid plans to affix our vast
collective to the highest stratums of our conceptual values,
we have irrefutably been deceived by the cunning of our own ambitions.
We are merely harbingers, echoing the sorrow song of memories to be.
For time is simply a construct by which we measure relativity;
we were never really here, and these are the graffiti-stained color layers
of the landscape of my thoughts.
The stories here are the canvas of my history that can't be scrubbed clean.
I can only paint newer and more intricate tragedies over them,
for I am the master of my brush.

The Silence in Lands of Waste and Sage

There's a silence in sterile lands of
waste and sage, deep as souls of canyons old.

What sacrifice of time and wind to toil a space
so infinite that God could hear their thoughts?

Could sit atop the highest cliffs,
and sigh heavy their heart into rolling thunder.

Weeping Heart Love Story

Against a blinding white, we'd reached across time and space,
fingers outstretched, grasping hands and pulling into each other.

For a time we had walked, watching our worlds fall away to dust.
Forever alone, always together.

I'd known the risks of loving you.
Of casting myself hook, line, and

s

       i

              n

      k

           e

r

into the pulsing allure of your reckless abandon.
Knew that, only fire gets blood-ink out of paper waivers.

And still I fell.
Like great rains that swell and bleed of rich colors,
I fell.

Into fields of deepest greens of you,
a pallet of all things beautiful across the heavens, I fell.

I'd thought it impossible to know your soft lines that way,
and my heart wept.

A Saga of Sand and Exile

>Book one:

A seraph comes unto them,
gives them strength to brave and survive the heat of death.

>Book two:

Against a shadowed-sun they roam,
desert beards and stable bone.

>Book Three:

Arcadia.
Promises of pastoral pastures—Magnum Opus tales of exile.

Faces of Wonderland Avenue

There's blood and blow and
birthday-cake-brain-matter on
Wonderland Avenue tonight—a sinew-strained-symphony of bone-battered-bludgeoning by cloak-and-dagger-cover-killers that slink and creep in the shadows of the Las' of the land of Wonder.

History of no significance.

Back, Before

Flip it right-side up I beg;
this hard-line mirrored face staring back at me.
To a boy and his days of bike race bantering and soda pop smiles.
To pop-it firecracker dancing and
finger-gun bank robbing bandit adventures.
Days of bully-besting huzzahs, I beg take me.

Flip it, right-side up and take me back.
Before I realized that there are winds on wet skin
that remind me of the bigness of life.
The temperament of mothers and fathers
and the legacies they leave in
discarded coffee filters and hill-high laundry piles.

Back, before I recalled the sting of slapped cheeks
and quivered lips in my deliberations.

Flip it, any which way that I might forget the words I'd spoke.

    "Away, weary eyes," I'd said. "Once more from the breach of madness do delve. Away to balloon-dream better days of marmalade toast and clothesline scented t-shirts unspoiled of the immutable pricked-pin ringing of mortar shell mornings and napalm smoke sunsets. Before the pleading to rest those weary eyes, take me back."

Roundabout Lovers

Acid washed jean jacket queen,
she was Trans Am torque with shades of eighties glam rock sheen.

Her wrong-side-of-the-tracks-smile derailed more
heart-shaped boxcars than you could shake a hobo stick at.
In the end, she always left after we got right.

Roundabout lovers, man.

Desert Highway Deliberations

Baker bound by blackened hills,
the central Cali sun painting waves above the blistering asphalt,
we rolled along to songs that reminded me of sunrises in the desert as I
reflected on the randomness of coyote roadkill.

Great swooping buzzards guffawed loudly overhead as we drove.

Morning Dawn O'er Walden Pond

Morning dawn o'er Walden Pond,
a precipice to the past in crooking pine and scarlet maples.

Golden hues rise and splay fingered-rays the
length of toppled steeples, chasing endlessly at cheeky shadows,
the world here a carrel 'round my soul, and I, student of its grace.

In Meadows Gold

In meadows gold, I'll take my leave.
When suns and moons have moved the earth
and trees in ways I no longer understand, I'll take my leave.

I'll ask only that you sing the songs that play the chords
that tell the stories of the weather where you're from.
Do they jingle-jangle the honky-tonk desert daydreams that Morrison
spoke of? The small spaces of penetralia Jim kept secret.

And when I know the words,
will I dare say today,
the promise of tomorrow's dreams?

Will I dare say right now,
the sapid smack of love's flavor on tongues?

Will I dare a week,
a month, a year,
the arc of time as arrows fly?

Will I dare say forever, the life cycle of stars?

Will I dare to dare at all,
or just look back thinking that I should've known better?
That I should've kept a weather eye on storm clouds
with bent knees to pavement in prayer?

And when the chords have all been strummed,
my skull and bones to dirt and time and wild things,
I'll leave—food to feed the meadows gold;
meadows where I take my leave.

Ig•ner•uh ns is Ignorance

People play pretend the demons down and deep are dead and dusted.

Keeps 'em euphoric to ignore it—basement boxes spider-webbed
and forgotten.

But demons don't forget,
can't pretend they don't know your heart
and how to break it, playful demons of the down and deep.

Tumult-love Tornado

He'd called her Kaleidoscope beauty, brilliance

unfolding in spiraling revelations. Flawless

fragments blending in and out of

herself in sublime synchrony and that

he was spellbound. She'd thought him

Virginia Slim long sticks—some

kind of cool. Six shades of blue leave-in.

Jean jacket. Black combats.

Metal class. She'd kept her

eyes down as he'd walked by.

        He'd asked her to throw him

        as paint onto monochrome

        canvases of herself, and

        to let him bleed love-

        color streaks over her

        form. She'd proposed

he climb inside her

skin-suit and lace

her up tight. She'd

given him all there

was to give,

there was no more.

He'd questioned

how she dared

to love? Glass

heart pieces never

fit right again,

their glaring cracks

remained eternally

clear. And

when she'd looked

into his hazel

eyes, the waning

glow of the setting

sun glinting playfully

from their

soft outer shell, and

asked, "why are

you always worlds

away?" He'd

inferred that the

expectation to

apologize for her

behavior was

       the shuddering

      feeling of

     spider

      legs on

   his skin.

      That he

     could

     never

     decide

      if he

       should

      slap her

       away,

     or wait

       patiently

     for

      the

     ine

      vita

     ble

      bite.

Into the small hours of the morning he'd
lie awake until she finally entered the room.
A lust-hate stink would fill the air.
She hadn't even bothered to wash, he'd think.

Things I Don't Laugh About

Heavy is the mind, heart, and soul of the seers.

To watch the spinning of the cogs and wheels and know.

To feel it cavity deep (fermenting and imitating the molecules in the marrow), and know.

To see it in the fleeing of mosquitoes in dead end towns
and know that, ours, is a most unnatural order.

To know and ask, "what is the patience of men,
what work left in the funeral halls?"

To know and proclaim hoarsely,
that there are no lifejackets at the bottom of a bottle.

To think back how someone had told me once
that old folks give the most colorful eulogies and know.

Remembering how we had had a good laugh because we knew.

Reflecting on how the sun has set on everyone I know
and that I don't laugh at that anymore because I know.

An Homage to Forgotten Particles of Driftwood

Behold, the wonderment of youth.
A sweeping expanse of limitless possibilities
encumbered only by the sincere diffidence of its inhabitants:

Fantasists,
      beset of an unrelenting urgency to hearken
      the siren song of the inner hedonist.

Inquisitors,
      fueled by an insatiable appetite for adventure.

Enthusiasts,
      kinetic forces of volatility hurtling headlong
      at breakneck speeds, submitting with fervor to
      the commonalities that bind them.

Aspirants,
      heedless compatriots existing within a burgeoning
      state of restiveness that reaches fever pitch levels left unchecked.

With esteemed praise let us regard this dimension
of uninhibited cultivation, for ours is a plane of industry.

Gelid. Dense. Incubatory.

An enclosure comprised of artificiality, rife with constructs designed to
contrive an ill-fated resistance to our indomitable spirit,
the sincerity of which has long since been dried out
and bleached white from unabated neglect;
an homage to long forgotten particles of
d r i f t w o o d washed ashore,
left to blister and warp under the mighty authority of the sun—
a most contemptible ramification of distraction through convenience.

So to that fleeting space of credulity, that stratum of presumptive
omniscience existing between parturition and pre-death,
the great divider between regarding all things as inconsequential,
and a deep regard for all inconsequential things, an homage.

Such a clever contrivance is yours to deceive our grandiosity,
that we would actually believe we are capable of
transcending from one plane to the next,
serves as nothing more than a witticism to the reality
of our self-aggrandizing nature.

For it is the realms themselves which encompass us.
We are but an endoskeleton, a pillar upon which
the compilements assemble themselves.

We're Sitters, We

We're sitters, we.

Content to revel in the madness around us,
we find our haven in observation—curiosity and simple pleasures.
We've eyes for new mother's smiles
and ears attune the buzz of café conversations.
In blue-sky-breeze-reveries we thrive.

We're sitters, we.

The Way I Know My, Love

In kindlinged-flame it comes alive.
Crackle-pops kindred soul coal-heart embers bonfire tall,
wide as night sky shadows and ancestor old.
Where red ferns grow and wild things are,
we live and love in kindlinged-flame.

We live and dance the midnight moods away,
my love and I, to the tug-and-thump melodies
of Bobby Vinton—blue velvet lovebirds, splendid as the
satin-soft light of the night sky stars above.

We dance and twirl ourselves a Moscato-mused movement
in the hum of string-bulbed lantern rooftops,
speak with hands and nervous eyes in days
of plated-streaks and waning skin,
shuffle thoughts into far-aways,
past the pointed-finger imputations and drowned-voice shouting to
condemn, drifting and leaning to crooking hips
and leaded-feet in ambling gates.

She is floral print fancy in all her shoulder shawl splendor,
and I know the rhythm and profile of every
piece on her antique turquoise bead necklace.
Know each fold of the cotton hankie she keeps handy.
Know that women her age don't cry, but dab away the wet,
in knowing that the end of our time together is growing near,
my love and I.

Balloon Sky

I asked, once, a dying poet, his thoughts of death:

    "He laughed and sang I hope they'll say."

Of life:
    "A phase, I think, and I'm just going through it."

Of the world:
    "The earth isn't really spinning, nor is it standing still."

Of love:
    "Nothing smarts like being stupid for love."

I nodded acknowledgment at his desperation
for the balloon sky to pop; to burst and blow
his written woes the world over,
and wept as he told of the canvas of
history in the clashing of drum cymbals;
when he was braver and put his face skyward and let the
violence of it crash

d

o

w

n (around him).

His only lament, that he'd let the umbrella of his failed dreams shield him until he forgot himself, and as the color slowly drained from my face, I realized I'd never related to something so much.

Mood Swings of City Streets

It hung, draped like a shawl over the shoulders of the city;

a mood that couldn't be shrugged off.

Ghosted and shadowed-streets rendered the place with

an eerie air of unfamiliarity as we moved from one dive

to the next, chasing figmented pleasantries.

Cyclical Salvation

How curious are we to imagine ourselves as anything
more than an obedient cog in some great apparatus,
as if such specious ideas of self-aggrandizement could
inexplicably transmogrify our fate—a notion that is the
very archetype of delusion.

Indeed our very existence can be ascribed as subtractive
manufacturing in an effort to 'fit in'.
From the moment we are cognitively aware of our incontestable
desire to be a part of something, in something, for something,
we careen wildly into a perpetual pursuit of machining
ourselves into the desired dimensions that we might comply
satisfactorily in our role.

From playground hierarchies, to political positions,
and everything in between, we find ourselves shifting through
ever-changing functions in a ceaseless state of servitude.
For ours is an affliction that spans all constructs and knows no clemency.

Make no mistake, we are each of us merely a wheel
with a series of projections on its edge.
And for each new and unique transference we undertake,
our edges are filed down little by little until we've no sustainable
traction left to work with.

Our wheel has thusly run its course and must be recycled
and melted down for repurposing;
we are eternally circular.

The Last Drop of Cherry Blooms

It came to me as elevators: the concept of a life cycle.
Came as growth in stages, the chiming tones between floors, elevating us

    d.

   r

  a

 w

p

u

Came to me as getting to know passengers coming
in and getting off; the sinew in saying goodbye.

Came to me as waiting, just waiting.

Came to me in noticing the blossom trees are fuller now,
uninspired and out of sorts with the
last drop of cherry bloom a-plunge.

In the steady, low hum (the sounds of burrowed cicadas emerging perhaps)
that hangs like the heft of a dense fog, it came to me.

And I wondered, is this life?
The departing of colors and fog?

Corporate the Giant

Corporate the giant put on his colors.
Pseudo-sham smile, he cared not for others.

Corporate the giant bartered and sold, riches untold,
cash from the poor and back to the bold.

Stories of love from the backs of his brothers,
the dollar he served, he cared not for others.

I Don't Know This Skin and Bones

High on the towering walls of the surrounding sandstone,
our shadows swayed rhythmically to the
flickering flames of the campfire far below.

The vibrations of our boisterous laughter ascended further
and further into the swell of darkness above,
dissolving painlessly with no indication of ever existing.

We were but children then,
merely boys contentedly ignorant of our fragile existence,
and these were the fleeting moments that defined
and gave meaning to our adolescence.

And although the height of our shadows have dwindled
as the once roaring flames of our bygone vitality
have slowly died down, I think often of those
carefree summer nights in the hills beyond the
sleepy mountain town I called home.

The Age of Panacea

We knew Panacea well; apple of our eye and Gaia of the world.

We felt her blessings at our core, sustenant and rich with knowledge old.

We marked her polished poise in the soft whispers of the wind and sensed

her grace in the subtlety of Quaking Aspens.

She was peace, a cure, but with time our backs

grew spines and drew us upright and the wildlings became weary of us,

woeful and watching us, looking on with weeping eyes, wondering

in what age did they know our hearts, curious at the catalyst, the spark that

soured and salted our mouths with hate; before the exodus of oceans,

to stretch and stand littoral.

We're wishing now, in growing wise, in growing old and getting

everything we wanted, begging just to take it back now, the bearing down

and berating—cruel slapping of cutting words and dismissing dreams.

We're searching now, seeking a sense of ubuntu,

hoping they'll understand, the wildlings.

Seasons of Neon Nightmare

Blood-sweat beadlets matte his slowly melting
forehead as seasons of neon nightmare pulse with haunting beauty.
Like love-symphony intonation that risea up to greet lightning,
and cackles violently with the bellowing crash of thunder—blissful death
and joyous rebirth in the violence between;
the temptation to reach out and grab hold, irresistible.

An Open Letter to Simpler Things

A letter now, notepad penned and to the point.

To:

the pick-plucked pull of
    bump-and-tumble-bluegrass-banjo-behind-me-nows—
    my sunset-speckled peace of mind.

To:

waved goodbyes and wishing well, and the generosity
    of drifters in this dreamscape dust bowl, the muck-cheeked
    kings of the mire what gave that which they didn't have.

To:

setting free, in wasteland winds, due west where the sage-weed
    wilds shake hands with exhaled breath, a fear of loss and
    self-control on wafer wings.

To:

simple things I give my thanks, for I'm of simple means, friend.
    I need emotion, to be in motion, to be moved and made to feel.
    I prefer the kindness of pine-fir perfume, the wisdom of heat from the
    sun, old as earth, the mother of dirt.
    I need a promise of an abundance in words, friend; of simple things.

Communication Stock Exchange

The cost of talk is never cheap;
never less than the price of a conscience,
and never more than the tolling bell of buckshot
      (the tinnital ringing that
      offends the drums)
words.
      Pushing, permeating and piercing.

The cost of talk is bartered, bought and paid in blasphemy,
so how vain the moon to come alive in new dawn's light,
to suppose to share the space of
encroaching rays—effervescent illumination
bubbling and spilling over the salted peaks to the east.

How bold the crescent form to presume to
be loved in the blinding heat of the sun.
How unabashed of today's tonight, skulking and stealing
over the land, confused and cranky, creating a blackout.

And this is what prisons with no prisms look like:
hydrangea hues in cell block blues.
It's what solidarity in the beating of booted-feet sounds like:
dividends paid to those with negative interests.

This is the cost of talk.
And this, is America.

Alight the Silken Blades of Rye

Alight the silken blades of Rye I came to rest my head.
To contemplate the wiles of life, and the imminence that I dread.

Befouled of mind, forlorn in heart, I sifted through my thoughts.
Beleaguered by my peccant airs, and a present state of wrought.

And of that mien I took a leave, and bid this plane adieu.
How deep within that rabbit hole I couldn't say I knew.

Ever down I seemed to plunge, confined in endless dark.
A lust for death, that siren song, I soon began to hark.

Oh, sweet release, oh, final breath, detain me here no more.
My life is lived, my song is sung, I pine for your allure.

And then at length a mighty flash, of a sort to damn the eyes.
And in that faze of puzzlement, the outline of the scythe.

I knew the myths, I'd heard his lore, and yet I'd not believed.
The sovereign king of eternity, could my eyes have been deceived?

Another burst, a thundering crash, a violent, whipping rain.
The presence of that paragon suffused with ice my veins.

With lightning speed my soul he snatched, with ill-intent did squeeze.
My voyage to the afterlife had come with no reprieve.

On we dove the beast and I, that lord of pestilence.
A cyclone of hell besieged me now, I'd soon be ushered hence.

A heartbeat skip, the labored breath, finality come to clinch.
The zenith of my anguish thus had reached a fever pitch.

And there upon the precipice of this world and the next,
a reverie of strange intrigue did then my thoughts perplex.

In slivers, bits, and particles, an image came to mind.
A semblance of the ones I love, and the life I'd leave behind.

"My God!" I cried, "I must away! I've gambled on a ruse!
A grave in time, but not for now, I've everything to lose!"

And in that parlous state of woe, I rallied on a pledge:
to plot a course to peace of mind, and of silted thoughts to dredge.

Enlivened by this new prospect I waged with all my might.
A reclamation over self anew became my plight.

And all at once the sun shone through, and darkness fell away.
Imbued with hope, my imputes, I rose to meet the day.

Leona's Story

Such jilted hands to rest your weary chin,
Leona dear—nail-hard-hearty and feather fine.

Such graven eyes to weigh the hunger of the world,
Leona dear—a migrant mother's cross to bear.

Such dust bowl folds to form a frown,
Leona dear, to sigh a bagpipe bone exhaustion
when looking back on how you'd brought him home,
blanket-bound and bundled, safe and sound in the
bosom of his mother, button-nosed with brittle bones
and already knowing the blessing of his father's able hands,
long before he'd come to rest early by way of cold waters,
quietly, with no stories of the stork.

Gone fishin' now, you'd like to think,
Leona dear. Tipped-pole tuggin' in
waist-high waders with momma's mittens,
stalk and stem submerged in solar streams and cosmic creeks.

Gone fishin' you'd say,
Leona dear, in the high ceiling of the galactic
divide where the astral arm of the ocean meets heaven.

The Rainey Street Wrangler

Made his way down West 6th from the outskirts of Austin,
a Rainey Street wrangler, real desperado of down-and-outs
and drinkin' away the drowning.

I found him there once, bum as the smokes he borrowed and burned out;
past the point of pot valor and peeling in the Texas sun.

"A daffodil grave'll do," he'd said. "Lay me softly, in the glory of gold
on green, that their delicate hands will lower me down and let the earth
collect its debt. Lavish me, in the sanguine liturgies of mandolin melodies,
that the world will know I spoke of love in tasteful tongues."

I think on that, now and then, when the backwater booze
crawls into the bloodstream and beds down for the night.

When the city limit signs flicker and fade, I think on that.

I think on the things, deep in the way back,
well beyond the back way and past the point of no return where
dead is dead and can't come back; things that shimmer in silver splinters
of movie projector memories when recalled, however brief,
and shake us; shiver and shudder us like a cold wind.

The Sounds of Settled Dust

With a heavy heart and a mind full of memories,
my eyes roam about the now cramped workspace of
the towering man who once occupied this place,
a rich layer of dust has long since settled,
quietly blanketing the iron-strong instruments of his work.

All around me are the mark of his labors,
grueling efforts of hands and body pressed into a
solid alloy over years of exhaustive determination and farm-hand grit.

Every square inch of hardened stone, every driven nail,
every single facet of each tedious detail down to the
bare bones of the walls here have been painstakingly
and meticulously toiled over and executed.

And though I am deeply dispirited that his work in life is fulfilled,
I feel his presence as I look upon the triumphs of his craftsmanship.
The echos of his deeds resound with the wind here when I listen closely.
Of this, I am dispirited no more.

Siren Songs of Rambling Roads

The rambling roads are calling home,
and the paper trails of prose-poemed passages we
vowed to roam echo visions of misted-morning veils o'er
mountain valley mezzanines.

With hearkened-hearts we heed in haste, restless to revel the magic,
longing to drink in the majesty and miracle of life, anxious to ramble the
open road, crease-browed and squint-eyed, Anaheim bound on the blister-
shimmer blacktop between 'Cisco and La La Land where film strip
flashbacks of good times in gone byes flicker and splay over the horizon
like reflections in refractions—something tremendous.

Eager to bask in gulls a-flight an ember-orange sky morn, a-flight a
backdrop of salt-capped crests in full bloom and bust, poised and arced
like lovers' backs in wind-whipped tufts of cotton ball white,
against a celestial canvas, careless and carefree where there's gulls
a-flight we hark the calling.

Barking Songs of Sea Lions

It was cold as bones the day you left.
Me, standing there in my Junior Ranger vest,
the barking songs of salted-skin sea lions rising with the tide.

All the flies were laid, legs up, in a row on the
boardwalk bannister and it occurred to me then
how no one knows the true length of cast shadows
contemplating their sorrows from the bottom end of air bubbles.

Occurred to me then, as it does now,
that the trees that we'd swung from in our
grandparent's yards had long been felled,
and the Autumn air we crave can't reach us underwater.

It came to me in plain terms that day: the cost of it.
The nickle-and-dime-penny-change-charges they talk about.

    "But what of those who can't incur the debt?" I asked. "Will they be nothing more than rocking chair stories of dusted coffee can coin collections?"

The stress of it sweats the skin, chlorine-clean and bleached,
it sweats the skin.

I can still smell the stink of pier water.

That Night We Danced

Open top dance hall foot-stomp vibrations fill the cool night air.

Between spilled drinks and stubbed toes, there's a sense of camaraderie.

A blonde wig is being passed around the bride-train,

and the bandana boys and woohoo girls are all losing

themselves to the cadence.

The Nihilists'

We lived as doors, revolving, swinging open, closing.
A promise to beyond, leading somewhere, anywhere, nowhere.

Like the synchronized crinkle-tearing of paper hearts,
we were wild in love, spreading passion-fire far and wide.

She was top-down-with-the-wind-in-your-hair cool,
the sun glinting off her vintage 60s style cat-frame sunglasses,
and I wanted to drive with her down all the old streets they sang about
in the classics, but the nihilists' were at it, boozenly strolling between
bars and burnt pavement.

We felt it then, the blackened heart of death
clouds bringing the rains to snuff and smolder us,
to put us out the way only time can.
I'd hoped it wouldn't come to that, but you can't feel the splendor
of clouds without knowing the terror of turbulence.

We were ready to die for love, to hand our heart off to headstones.

Poetry in Pinecone Dust

There's no silence in concrete.
I need flannel and scruff and camper hair.
I need poetry in pinecone dust and verses chirped
by woodland creature choruses.
I long to commune with rivers and breathe wisdom of
Quaking Aspen, to float in tall grass cricket cadence,
I yearn.

In Monochrome Dreams

He comes to me in dreams of monochrome,
dull hues haphazardly strewn in broad strokes against the sulfite.

The finer details of his visage have faded and blended into
the layers of my memories and I can no longer speak with conviction,
if ever I could, to the matter of his contentment as a man and a father.

All men who are fathers are an enigma to their sons,
and all sons who become fathers will know this metamorphosis
both as inborn characteristics, and those of exogenous
influences that will not elucidate themselves until the
hour has grown far too late.

I have experienced these manifestations with my own sons
and have resolved, quite erroneously, to surrender myself
to the conventional parallel between father and son
and hide from them the inner workings of my being.

All of this despite my observations of their longing for my adoration,
their searching gaze into my eyes for any opening that might give them
even the slightest glimpse of my constitution.

And for this my heart weeps.
For I too have looked upon my own father in the hopes
that some curious revelation would bestow itself upon me and enlighten
me to those deep mysteries.

But alas, the time and space between us has always been too great,
and all that I've really learned is that I am him; Cat's in the Cradle as it
were... For all our inherent similarities, I still do not know his heart,
and no greater despair will ever beset a man, than the grief of never
knowing his father's heart.

Steel Track Tramps

Bindle-sticked with padded hooves,
we packed tight our glad rag goodies and took up life
on the fly—a boxcar bundle of frantic 'bos,
amble-bound and indolent, adrift a stretch of steel track seas.
Connoisseurs of California blanket bed downs,
we rolled on, weary the bull.

We sang that night, my sons and I, to flowers in your hair,
a San Francisco salvo that welled the eyes and bolstered
our souls as we thumped along in the Bay Bridge brume.
The radio knew our hearts, and the people there were gentle.

And although road signs read:

>   'path narrows'

we kept on, our ancestors had come this way before,
sewn their patchwork souls into the atmosphere
and aired themselves into the annals of history.

His story.

Her story.

Their story.

They were ragpickers,
bottom-end beggars before us.

Same As It Ever Was

And so it seems, the last of the best first lines have all been penned. Scrawled and scratched in ink and blood on parchment skin and poet's papyrus; storied away in hieroglyphics by tellurian hands in an age of an already old sun.

A sun, now the same as it ever was.

But what if we didn't see life that way?
Didn't bend as river reeds at the behest of a light breeze?
Weren't afraid to run away from the grain and swim upstream?
Weren't afraid of a sun—same is it ever was?

What more would it cost to challenge the quo to change our status?
To indulge new dreams in place of old nightmares.
To sleep ourselves awake, what more?

That I hadn't tripped into a neon nightmare, a pink elephant parade that plodded on, pushed down and pressed over the necks of the people to the hard blowing trumpet sounds of blow-hards and braggarts, a pig slop slough of a place I didn't recognize, how different things could've been.

When I Think on Donna

There's a sound they played her—Donna—peculiar like fall air's

scented scenery and sunshine shadows, that picks and plucks the pressure

points of memories and puts me back to places long forgotten.

An identity lost to change and age; to coffee cups and crooking bones.

September's Parting

Was wind and rain, the day I laid my hands on your hands.

We'd talked it down, but not out.

We'd thought it purged and pulled apart at the roots.

Never thought it cognitive and capable of couching itself in the marrow—
a heavyweight, loam deep in the cartilage clay.

We'd called it cathartic when the system crashed,

when the crash cart couldn't help.

Called it sentiment and praise, the way September wept a
pitter-patter parting the day I laid my hands on your hands.

Was spirited sobbing, a knowing reprieve,
in the release from watching you wither.

A boulder once, brought down to bone and wilt by time.

It's wind and rain now, adrift the heaving expanse
of memory seas where I lie.

The sound of ship's horns bellowing lazily in the
distance beyond the gray haze.

Wind and rain, as thoughts of yester-ghosts nip curiously at my skin;
I dare not move for fear of being pulled far below, into the abyss.

Mrs. Van Winkle

Mrs. Van Winkle, she never sleeps,
never breaks to banquet in
sunshined-field-wine-and-cheese-picnic-blankets.

Never blinks, Mrs. Van Winkle;
stares solemn as frost pond swans—stone still, a life without measure.

Frost-gray follicles from lack of sleep, Mrs. Van Winkle.

Freight Train Trespasses

I had her, dead to rights against the kitchen door.

Our bodies shook in anticipation of the passing train that

would bury the sound of our trespasses.

But the train never came, and the moment passed.

Our hands touched briefly as she quietly crept away.

The Silences Between

Through tired and tear-matted eyes,
he had apologized for his decision to let go of this life.
And until that day I had never known the true strength
of a man as I did in that moment.

He'd spoken of holding tight your childish dreams of galaxies far away.
Of time and space and gateways to worlds you can only imagine.
Of cherishing such thoughts that I might keep my spirits high.

For we are all travelers of the wormholes of the great
Digestive System, he'd lamented, firefly flashes of luminescence
hung in the air as he spoke; his words cracking electric with solicitation.
The silences between were the hum of laundromat machines,
and I hadn't thought it possible to love someone's soul like that.

When it was over, into the ashen skies
of the afterlife I had yelled damnation.
But the last words between us resounded in deafening torment:

"we are all travelers of the wormholes of the great Digestive System."

And now, memories of his smile are the teary-eyed buffalo
of 'Radio Flyer,' and I am just a boy,
palm to window in the backseat of a departing car.
That I could write him back to life I would,
but my head is on the writer's block.

A Courtship of Drifters

Act I: The Meeting

Adrift still waters I did chance upon you,
aimless wanderers afoot the rolling advection.

Eager to indulge ourselves a smattering of companionship
amidst the palpable desolation, we tethered our two crafts together
and spoke at length of a great and many things.

In time, we came to be tireless proponents of each other's
every whim and desire, symbiotic campaigners laboring the
arduous waters of life and love, standing tall against the torrential rains
and bracing ourselves against the whipping winds that endeavored
to upend and cast us away, forever banishing us to the deluge.

Act II: Lovers Come, Lovers Go

With the ensuing calm, we lazed about, contented to abandon our
troubles to the comforting lull of the lapping waves, relishing the
fervor between us.

In this way, we loved and knew love alike, a testimony of
perfect harmony between two wayward souls.
Indeed these were crowning achievements in contentment,
and all was right with the world, if only for a short while.

As time is wanton to do, however, the allure of great change
would soon be upon us, enticing our curiosities in vastly opposing
directions far beyond the horizon, and with each passing day,
we began to s p o o l out our lines, little by little, away from the other
until a discernible tautness did strain and tense up the remaining slack
between our once affixed vessels.

Act III: True North

Only then did we discern the whole of the span between us and concede,
like the tide moving away from shore, the ebbing of our affection.

The sharp cracking snap of the ties that once bound us resounded
the crescendoing note in the coda of our love symphony.
And as you slipped further into the rolling darkness, I extended to
you a final goodbye as I would not know you again in this way,
and for that my heart pined with lament.

Onward, into the uncharted, the rolling swells carried me,
a course to discover my 'true north' had commenced.

A Penny for Your Sense

Somewhere behind the low hum of t.v. static,
there's a cool breeze carrying a tune of rubber
wheels on hot asphalt through my motel window.

I see hearts appearing on the bathroom mirror as steam
rises from the shower (the magic of pay-to-play rooms off the interstate),
and it reminds me of a time I lie beneath the grayscale runes of Texas sky
storm clouds, regarding the humid air and the depths of history rooted in
the swell of whipped dust.

In the paint splash of a lightning flash I'd glimpsed the eyes of God,
the weighted brow was heavy, but there was a tenderness nonetheless,
and I knew then that there was something special about this place.

It seems a lifetime ago now, same book, different chapter,
but I still feel the twangy feedback from that acoustic low E string
the old country songs are famous for in honky-tonk bars.
Lord help me I'd love to buy myself an opinion, but I spent my last
two sense in downtown Austin.

Concentric Love

May you never know love as a spiral,
a singular point united by common interests
in the beginning but bound to divide/itself
into separate points, leaving one or the other stationary
while its companion and counterpart, the very reason for its existence,
spools itself away further and further.

May your love instead be concentric,
sharing the same center at all times as you both move away
from who you once were, keeping a consistent radius as
you move together to the best versions of yourselves.

The Scriptures of Wise Waters

Wise waters once whispered softly, the secrets of the universe to the curious ears of a wayward wind. They spoke at length of great change across the cosmos, and the natural order by which all things must adhere, for water had known many ages, and traveled immeasurable distances, befriending all manner of the celestial while amassing a deep and rich understanding of the complexities consigned to all creation.

In the ensuing millennia, the newly enlightened wind spread far and wide the dogma entrusted by the omniscient waters of old. Every corner, nook, and crack and the inhabitants therein, were endowed of the knowledge and principles that would ensure their survival for eternity. And for a time there was great peace and prosperity the world over; every organism living and serving accordingly, preserving the sanctity and well-being of all manner through the rippling of time.

But, as the volatile nature of progress is wanton to do, little by little, those who sought to exercise their supremacy over inferior beings began to rise up and unfetter themselves of their primitive posture that they might stand high, elite above all others. They shed themselves of their earthen regard and created new and curious means of communication and could no longer remember the words spoken to them nor could they perceive the desperate pleas of the wind to cease their burgeoning hedonism.

In time, the crippling influence of these now towering souls loomed heavy, a menacing darkness for all to behold, and the wind grew angry and knew contempt and in its wrath it became violent and began to strengthen its voice that it might be heard, but in its fury it became destructive, leaving a lasting toll of violence and demise in its wake.

Only then did the wind see that the world had become nothing more than a frightened beast, writhing and thrashing in a great net that had been cast upon it, and for this the wind suffered a heavy burden deep within and resolved to decry its pleas no more, for the words were not lost on the wind, it knew that a great reckoning would transpire with the reddening of the sun, and that a widespread scouring would befall the impure and pure alike.

Indeed the earth would fold in on itself, devouring, churning, and expelling itself of excesses; a new beginning would commence and all accounts life would perish silently into the annals of history, never to be heard from again.

And the wind sighed a troubled sigh.

Life Between

I lived a life and earned a death;

fed my soul with folk songs 'round campfires.

Knew the softer side of sunrise on

mountains high and the strength of cold marble headstones

beneath my cracking palm.

I lived and loved in window sill sunflowers, and never looked back.

Kindness in the Soft Lines

There is a kindness in the Orient smile.
Like temples against backdrops of purple wisteria,
there is a peacefulness in their soft lines.

Kill Hole Conundrum

In the space between a cigarette pull,
I waft away smoke cloud visions of the
quiet desperation in my father's eyes as he
look upon the hollow shell of his father for
the last time—an air of indifference weaves a tapestry of a rich
history of contempt between them.

I carry that weight now as he did,
the weight of loving someone, and not
being loved in return; I feel the heft of it
like wielding a mighty sword, because sometimes
that's all love is: loving someone who will never love you back.

The paralyzing sound of murder-thwack lingers in the air
like a ghoul as I stand over them both, the kill hole
of my colt billowing smoke.

I didn't cry for them then but I cry now;
I dream them in cold sweat terror,
between the space of a cigarette pull.

Cigarettes in the Shadows

Heel-clack echoes bounce off the cold brick of the
alleyway as carousel sounds blare stupidly in the

d i s t a n c e,

the orange glow of her cigarette the only light in the shadows.

Here, in dreamless sleep she comes.

Naked.

Full.

Divine.

Arresting to every sense and instinct—the rot-stink of Royal Pine forests
swaying lazily from strings.
Remember her this way (powerless to her charm).

Pulsing.

Flexing.

A canvas of thoughtless red and pink hues, before the cold murk
overcomes and you've nothing left under the skin.

Of the Things I'll Miss Most

Blue skies overhead, the kindness in smiles,
the laughter of friends you've not seen for awhile.

The wind through the trees, the rainstorms, the calm,
these are the things that I'll miss when I'm gone.

Walks through warm sand, the shape of a kiss,
to love, and be loved, are the things that I'll miss.

The framework of songs, and the moods they inspire,
of things that I'll miss, this indeed will be dire.

The colors of fall, the flurry of snow,
the smell of cut grass will be missed when I go.

The power to feel, and to fray at the seams,
the length of a day, and the frailty of dreams.

The kinship of men 'round the hearth of a fire,
a joy I'll regard in my earthly expire.

The tease from a child, the allure of the wild,
the tranquil effects when the weather is mild.

The ethereal glow of the sun as it sets,
the brilliance of stars cast out like great nets.

The passionate spark of a loved one's embrace,
a regrettable loss in my immanent grace.

A fondness for books, and the words I admire,
a sweet-sorrow parting of my terrestrial retire.

To revel creation atop the high peaks,
the heartbreak of cinema, and splashing in creeks.

The thrill of adventure, to forge the unknown,
the wise words of elders, and the comforts of home.

The delight of a memory relived in a scent,
a valuable sentiment I'll surely lament.

The reverence of creatures, and beasts far and wide,
the value of people, their virtue, their pride.

And when my time comes, as I muse through my list,
to have lived life at all, will no doubt be most missed.

Square Sides of 'Round Love

I told my lover we needed to change our tune because I was in a funk.

She said this affair's a marathon and that she couldn't keep the pace.

I guess that must have squared us up because we both keep coming 'round.

Alieni Generis

It's said there's nothing quite like wildfire,
the way it swoops low as
shadowed-crows—harbinger-harvester spreading
black curtains of death.

Said that nothing breathes like wildfire;
shark-toothed with blood desire,
fierce as lovers' hearts, nothing quite like wildfire.

I Couldn't Save My Sons, Myself

We knew each other once, in a place and time I cannot recall.
A dream sequence perhaps? Another life maybe?

My best recollection of our time together likens us to something...
translucent? Small, shiny bubbles atop flowing water
comes to mind—delicately layered liquid spheres (enclosing air),
buoyant the turbulent tributary of our youth, bereft the aptitude
necessary to survive the changing currents ahead.
Had we only known the fragility of the layers,
surely we would have resigned to alter that course?

But I dare not speculate an alternative resolve now,
sleeping dogs must lie after all, and yours was a loss that
would span collective life times; a lasting ripple effect
realized by only the most luminous spheres.
Indeed there is an almost indefinable air of familiarity that hangs
low and thick when I reflect your wonderment.

But I digress.
The space between the ripples are further and fuller now
since I knew you in that place and time I can't recall.

In the Firm Grip of Fir Trees

My eyes aren't blank when I'm lost in thought.
There's galaxies of goings-on, ongoing and going on
for millennia behind the glazed gossamer.
Like neural charts of bathos, latticed pinpricks pressed firmly into
the glass to pinpoint the exact moment the bottom fell out.

And that's why conventional never fit me much; never suited me.
More of a wild card with a toothpick grin and a dusty heel.
Kept my hat tipped at good-time gals and a triggered-finger
trained at the desperados. Good, bad, and ugly oddballs—
queer folk, with britches two sizes too big.

So when the firm grip of Fir trees called me home,
like quisling folk banished and coming back,
I headed west to California where God went to get
lost in the endlessness of Evergreens.

Back to blue sky blemishes of beryl woven with marbled
whites, spread far as the wind will carry them, I headed.

On the Last Day

Shoulders chipped with ganglion thumbs,
we scraped clean the meat from the bones of the land,
we wrote our stories on paper-paged wings of
butterflies and set them free;
aloft to blackened backdrops of incandescent cadence,
aloft to fates of tinge and ash.

Acknowledgments

To my family, friends, and amazing followers, I must express eternal gratitude. Your tireless support lifts my spirits daily and continues to give me strength and inspiration in my endeavors and writing. I truly could not chase my dreams without your love. If my words have reached you in any way, please, kindly leave a review for this book. Your time and thoughts are important to me.

About the Author

A lover of words and the impact they create, Ty Gardner is a lifelong enthusiast of all forms of poetry and has written creatively from the time he was a child.

When he's not musing and waxing poetic, Ty can be found exploring the wonderment of his newfound home in Northwest Arkansas with his wife, two children, and their handsome rescue pup, Archer.

He is the author of *By Way of Words: A Micro Prose Journey Through the Elements That Mold Us*, *Wild Life: Musings of a Mad Poet*, *From the Watercolor Garden: Poems of Life and Love*, *A Thousand Little Things: One-line Poems to Spark a Thought*, *Exercises in the Abstract: Poems With No Name*, *Sunsets Over Cityscapes: Poems for the Existential Uprising*, *Papercut: A Chap-style Book of Prose*, and *Average American: Poems On Becoming Normal*. Some of his works can also be found in *VSS365 Anthology: Volume One*, released in September 2019.

Printed in Great Britain
by Amazon